TAMBOURINE INTERWEAVE

POEMS

Rosalie Barci

Apostrophe Publishing
Finksburg, Maryland

Tambourine Interweave
Copyright © 1994 Rosalie Barci

Library of Congress
Cataloging in Publication Data
ISBN 0-964-3777-0-5

Published in the author's name by
Apostrophe Publishing
Finksburg, Maryland

Manufactured in the United States of America

Contents

Dedication

You befriended me -- we cultivated
each to give to the other.
No matter, I am your friend,
grateful to you because you are you.
Your needs are my needs, your sorrow
my sorrow, your happiness -- my joy.
I might not tell you sweetly that
you are my friend, nor do I always
respect your feelings when I am tired,
however, you are my friend.
I proudly applaud you and inwardly
and quietly wish you love.

****

Love Song

Sing and don't cry
because in singing
hearts are made happy.

****

The Woman

I met her. We spoke.
In her I saw someone dear.
She was patient with me and told me of herself.
She was old and when she spoke she reminisced.

The lines in her face were soft and smiling,
the delicate twinkle in her tired eyes told me
she was sad.

Frightened Reverie
A tear to fall between
Death-take her Not!

****

Not Blind Love

I look for you, you're not there.
I don't expect you any more,
I only wish and hope
someday we may find one another.

****

Yard Friends

Our small dog -- rust, brown and black.
She had one paw raised, stepped on a stack,
a stack I believe, piled in front,
went to see her companion and got foiled.
Foxy's friend was close to the wood -- May
got too near -- nothing misunderstood, however,
playfully they tangled.
The wood wasn't safe, only for fire.
Foxy's friend was a romper --
a turned up nose, cute, left a smell of earth;
the devil intervened.

The wood remains, Foxy limps, May has
departed, Spring has arrived.
With three feet she'll jump the fence --
one paw raised.
May has departed.
Petunias arrive, after the shower,
and Foxy as wild as the Dandelion is
back to four.
Spring and Foxy three-simply temporary.

****

Action Taker

I hinted --
the interest was there
the complete satisfaction was not
so my head said what I was thinking
under the influence of make-believe,
and trouble began anew.

****

Caring Love

Not from afar have I watched you;
I understood you like a mystery
wishing always to hurt you, then
suffering in silence with you.

****

Bound Sharing

Since I cannot find words enough
to tell you how I love you --
I am only then, to love you.
Love me.

****

Not to Do

Boredom likes lethargy --
lethargy boring deeper into boredom
to halt with a cog the wheel of
progress, thereby providing a standstill
gravely unable to bore past a stiff-
necked couch warmer unwilling to bend
the other way, hence not alleviating
energy sluggishness which settles
as a crafty, silken web of cob en-
circling around, tightening about --
like the harness gripping close
and checking tautly, only to
hinder grossly the buds of creativity
nurtured by movement, with
a wee bit more than a spurt -- as the
extension of an action; less of a
grumble and more of a grunt.

****

Building

Chalk it
Caulk it --
    fork spoon and knife.
Writing about chalking talk caulk
if in a walk
very often fulfills an emptiness
that brings satisfaction!

****

Mint Tea

Geometric design -- be it of green on tan
at the hieroglyphic sarcophagus in red
heat where life does not exist, save
but to see the sunset and adorn scarab.

****

His and Hers

Rompers and radicals,
both have fun,
alive and alert --
bar none.

Big and boisterous,
sound that horn --
romper and radical
less then some.

Serene and suave
they are the same --
frank and fruitful,
more then many.

Joyous and jolly
that they be --
luscious and lively,
less then we?

****

Fluff

Bunny rabbit in the barn,
bunny rabbit from the farm --
you make me happy when
I see you run.

Nibble, nibble wag your fluff,
make me happy, I am not rough.

A puff of Fluff --
your tiny tail,
Bunny rabbit, huddled bale.

****

One Only

Black baby, I love you so.
Black baby, so mean to me.
I want your love!
When you came I found the world.
When you left, I ached.
I was with one he gave me warmth,
another near -- he cared.
Oh! missed lover.

Black baby, hurting for you still, you
who left me longing for your roughness,
longing for your touch and tormented
for your kisses.
Your love words cut into my being like
my blood, like the ache
so sweet, so sweet --
so bad for me yet so good.

****

Rain Drape

I was beholding simple beauty
as the rain now falling heavily
surrounded Nature in a sturdy aura.

****

Persian Prince

My cat is like none other, I am
his only lover.
We play peek-a-boo and hide and go
seek, we run and we scamper and
we enjoy kissing cheeks.
We help one another by loving each other,
we keep our distance though -- he
permitting me, and, I permitting him
to catch with fun -- when we play
hide and seek.

Under the chair, he scurries away,
into the closet and I say nay.
Out, out, come let's go,
I'll find you and your hiding
place, then when you see me I'll
hide my trace.

****

In for Lunch

At times there is a wish to express
myself; thoughts get crushed with
ugly old memories of bad times and,
I'm delayed.
The ugly thoughts desire attention
they do not always receive. Damn,
up again -- bothersome delay, the
anger causing twice a put off
of reminders which loom at my time --
becoming distorted and occasioning
me the fool. Distraught, I dis-
tribute annoyance to a saucy lunch,
well undigested.

Perhaps setting my wits to work
and thinking of the odious indelible
things which force their way at me
I may make them acquaintances and,
will sufficiently ignore.

****

Provisional Glitter

A balding head and sparkling eyes hiding
behind an American Beauty Rose introduced
to the crowd -- so self-assured, so confident,
   ever so suave,
    a forging smile winning you friends.

I ended my white water conversation and
melted with interest at the lyrical accent
   I came to know, in time to grow with love.

   A war waged on --
seized by discontent holding fast --
   arrival of truth that love is liar
   to the heart.

****

Madrugada Dia

Yo te quiero me esposa, en la
luz del madrugada --
Yo te quiero.

****

Por Ustedes

Mi ninos, cada dia es nuevo
y alegre quando usted buscar
la estrella.

****

He Is There

He is there. So silent, so invisible
to my unseeing eye. I do not see,
But He is still there. He doesn't
speak -- He knows I err, am not perfect
yet I do know He loves me.
Sometimes I forget He loves me then,
I wonder if it is He who forgets and
I am lost. I seek them, He listens
to me silently.
When I speak openly to Him I realize.
He frustrates me sometimes because
I cannot touch Him. It is difficult.
His burden is not the same as mine --
I shall share. I hope to have calm
endurance and, remain in patience.
There is a tender Man.

****

The Rosebud of Love

I saw a child in my travels.
I stopped to say hello, however,
the child intervened with silence.
I became silent in awe --
As I smiled and said good-bye, I
watched his tiny fingers touch the
delicate rosebud.
You my little one, became my child.

****

Serenity...
   to you at this time
   and always

****

Words from May

Jeff and June --
puppy dog, pussycat.
Friends of each other,
-- companions of mine.

Every so often we cheerfully romp,
through the grass and around the stump.

The dinner bell jingles and we depart,
to our respective meals --
with a quick start.

We delight in refection
then set out again --
satisfying an important life,
breezes blowing; devoid of strife.

****

Express Round

when it comes to righting writing
do you care to right the writing
or is it wronging of rightness
that often foments a realm of
neglect only to foment the other??

****

Life Bird

Bird singing
Bird building.
Bird flying hither, away
to serenade the mate.

****

Sun Rain

Running water in the stream --
pebbles and rocks;
Sun-filled happiness and flying birds.
Trout frying over little round coals --
my friend beside me with a lazy look.

We climb those hills and speak of trout,
the hills become mountains but we are strong,
our senses delight and Nature abounds.
Fresh sweet air and warm sun --
daffodils daisies and dandelions
not few.

Mossy rocks, look! a brimming brook,
a pause to ponder the wonder of Life.
A tree growing
oh, so long ago -- earth so fertile,
earth that is mine.

No clouds do we see on a sun-drenched mountain,
reign on buttercups,
Nature is free.

Sudden to us, rain appears -- delicious
soft rain as it touches my face under
a sky of blue!

And, steadily now the rain falls deep.
We cannot continue as night also falls --
the tent that was pitched prepares us
for rest.

Pang -- the voice of the rain
lulls me to sleep; my friend the mountain,
in rain so deep.

****

Brew Days

Without a cup of coffee the day progresses to hell.
It rests in my hand, sits near, and remains my
bitter companion.
Refills of empty, cold or hot get drunk
with pleasure.
Tasty buds don't die with coffee being
my measure.

In my life it's in demand, always there, here,
and near.
I don't ring the death knell when coffee
is finished -- although my brain seems diminished.

For me it's best that I'm in un-hell,
I have a cup, in my hand it's pressed.

****

Undisturbed

No! Your clone I am not; your textbook
specimen -- an arrogant piece of frail work
I refuse.
You boast and gape in my face, reproach
your mind-game which survives to damage.
Inner love burglarized by impute
destroying and persecuting as you move
along like the parasite feeding,
and weakening.
Sight has left you, blind-lending itself
farther backwards to regress; a non-exit
imitating mistake.
Will applause tell you?
Interwoven ahead of Time is the progression
of Progress -- to us uncomfortable?

Mind's eye views the lantern bright in
speaking truth, where might be music,
love and beauty for all.

****

Indefinite Need

Desperate arms which damage,
Fiery lips tell rage --
Scourging eyes -- how they intimidate!
Lost hurt years remembered, in painful
tears.

****

Muse

My anger knew no boundaries when you
disappointed me
        with your absence.
I flew into a raging storm whose holocaust
        was the void.
Stifled by your inadequate behavior,
my salty tears petrified an already expressionless
beauty into one --
        a dreadful apprehension.

Vain remains beauty traveling on,
laughing at the absence, the holocaust
        in abeyance.
She is sick at heart yet rich in spirit,
for love fosters her strength.

****

Autumn Night Ride

Into the quiet of the starless night darkness
      gobbles us in its arms.
Enveloped within the grip of mighty timbers
      beneath a moon that lights the sky of
      October paths.
Mustangs carry kissing couples in a jouncing
      wagon scarce-covered of hay, complete with
      lovers and devoid of sound.
Wagon wheels bump us along in the cold night
      air, the ground covered over with frost;
      we are traveling -- cold lips warm and touch;
      the volume of giggles decreases and we
      remain close, peeking at passing pumpkins.

Lo! Witches accelerate, notch and dart,
      arresting any peeking -- heads turn as bats
      soar and jumbo phantoms hover above --
      spirits of the night riding everywhere.

Cuddling, frightened lovers hide down from
      crafty goblins and stare at the stage,
      the horrifying scene, eyes wide at
      hobgoblins dodged...
Silently holding each other along the trails
      of thickets; where is the missing hay?

****

Your Arrival

'Twas bitter December and I dream of July --
sultry days and going coatless.
I shop in my mind for sandals, short shorts,
and racy incidentals and cogitate about
breeze blown hair and thin gelatin desserts
and playing racquet-ball in outdoor courts
while I perspire; it keeps me stingingly
interested.
Quiet sands on Island moonlight beaches
where I slip nothing on and am delicious,
makes me impassioned.

Blizzard snows gust outside the window and,
I am waiting for July, my backside in freeze
stiff position fancies the nearness of
your love -- over hot soup, and dreamy
Lilliputian wine cakes.

****

Lovers

He loved her so dearly,
And she betrayed
Their most precious treasure
that time had made.
Now her heart is saddened
And the tears are near,
As she thinks of those
wonderful, happy years.

The years when their hearts
were carefree and gay,
And their love was expressed
in so many ways...

****

Organdy Love

MaMa of Bride shops not modestly
sturdily draped by bulging money holders
that shore up for sanctuary --
    and the Silver Castle stands tall.

Viceroy absentees signing off seats --
    far from genuflection.

Francais in sepia sounds choir organ
melody that quilt silky white organdy
bedecked aside -- outlets of horticultural
appeal meted generously for the few.

Promises spoken, composition love
shared, offering the future tread
    with care.
Hungry wedding night tenderness
journeying lovers to the borders
of paradise.

Non-defunct uninsured parallel parkers
in lots craving Christianity --
    Confetior, Confetior.

****

Gray Love

Oh, Splendor!
Grandeur not mine --
shown through your eyes, a look to kiss -- then
a growing uncertainness of loving tenderness?

Do you pretend a love sincere
which taunts my heart,
aching a truth of love.

****

Exchange

They speak --
he neglects her
she leaves him
they speak no more
Then, they do not speak again.

  Why do they quarrel?
  Do they care?

Do they not understand
to discover in gentleness?

****

Apart

Your love for me is there --
so subtly is it expressed.
We have spoken, together we have
shared, our silent secret moments that
only our eyes express? My love to not
cry and laugh alone -- not apart, not without.
Our moments --
Ever greeting each tenderness,
Ever to love.
A silence spoken.

****

Lovely Ballerina

They had delicate-looking faces yet their
strong and slender straight backs did not
suggest impatience, but, rather a calming
still loveliness as they chatted in poised
chignons.
China-like hands held rough hewn mugs; I
basked in their form, my mind wanders
to the far away gentle Volga flowing
naturally, quietly.
I could only think of beauty within their
grace -- charmingly alive, seemingly intricately
balanced in light conversation.

****

Journey

Circuitous monotony -- electrically blazing
paths beginning an end seizing each way.

Expectatious youth life, eagerness gesturing forth.

-- Almagamate dreams tunneled in memory
leading this way and that -- a particular apart.

Labyrinth attention -- the static semblance,
patterned faces sentenced at nothingness.

    "DESTINATION"   "DESTINATION"

       Racing stations cryptically transferring --
obliteration near, hither working.

DISCHARGE!   DISCHARGE!   DISCHARGE!

Now, stares offended to ebb with slumped ledgers
which defy satiation -- emptiness holding,
engulfing the hideous vacuum --
a junction of incensed pause.

****

Endless Escape

Stated monotones in seething anger, a myriad
of thoughts flooding his mind -- rapid, angry,
careful sensing a danger as the speaker speaks --
authority queries, in tongues unknown.
"You are wanted -- I must have you," in
voice staccato.
"Hear, here be the handcuffs -- it is
an arrest."
-- Unjustly taken failed information leading
him to a destination --
Where do they take him?
What words do they utter? They want ME?
They've come for ME?
Bastards! Bastards!
"You have the wrong person Sir --"
the idea you have is strange to me, my
innocence, it is innocence; not boxed in Sir --
liberty, freedom, Justice!
Is there no justice?
Why do you relate the crime to me?
Sir, this is psychologically painful and
humiliating, a thorn in my side is what you are!
"Yes I killed her."
Where do we go, my rights, my rights!
I have rights. Sir!

****

Boat House

The silent house on the water
The stillness of the air
The hush of rippling waves
(The) --pale softness to view,
The quiet in my mind
(The) place of your beauty,
The stumble of love --
   to greet where you are.
Two, together as we love.

****

Public Love

He is living --
perusing the tome.
I think I like him; he looks mean.
Perhaps I won't speak to him --
As he departs to his page with a
  glass to see,
I research the lines in his face and
go back to my book.

****

The Scoop

He comes across as a thief.
I spot him stealing from the sprinkle
  jar to attack an ice cream cone --
  then he runs from the cherry Coke
only to taunt me with wicked cream.
Taking the cake, he frosts a Happy Birthday.
Shaking of him -- if a lover knew.
A permit to go off the diet with sweet kisses
  and candy lips would be stirring,
A Big melt -- like the syrup of LOVE.

****

Dweller

I remember the stench
I remember desolation
I remember my home town.
Lonely avenues filled with few people all
   strange to me, stinking bodies breaking by --
   a sham a sham
Emptiness in tears, recalled with sadness,
a vulgar emptiness bearing itself upon the world
   of my home town.
I'll leave, desert this place forever!
   not tolerate emptiness and desolation
   nothingness to view.

A manic anger stirs in me ceaselessly to ask;
of what significance is my home town?

Simple silence wrecked in the mire of lonely decay
Aged minds in a world of secured death --
proper voices trembling competition knavishly
set to castigate.
Benign neglect with jealousy and mock scorn
departing from the bearer unto me -- the thorn?
Dulled senses --
Silent answers of the heart?

I remain generous in greed to resist, and take not
   the rotted words.

Custom awares self-logic, I henceforth leave
the trickster words to them, to be mine not.
I leave take the captive.

****

Response

Sweet lips that tease me so
with little response to you;
my love, forgive my aching heart
who longs to embrace you tenderly,
and with your kiss, tell you of my love.

****

Regarding Thee

Witty art thou with thine eyes
so full of love.

Hiding thy kisses with a medicine
so known to me.

Shalt thou be mine?
Oh, sweet mystery.

Wretched shall I be when the dawn
sees thee gone!

Leave me not to suffer an agony --
such as without thine eyes to see.

****

Roads of Time

Chowder quahog marshed in cruised canal
mingling sun memories

bustling bazaars walls winging retraced
treasured miscellany of unfolded importance

attendant auctions scattering
the canopy of golden leaves

theatre seats at Harbor Ice

Silent snows
to touch your body

sleeping Widows Walk
with Pavement of sleep --
leading me every which way,

Passing years and days after
of always -- roads of Time.

****

A Time to Dream

Thank You my love for teaching me,
  what true love is and really can be,
Although we two are forever apart --
You, my sweet will be always in my heart.

Your lips were warm
  I loved them so.
But now it seems, so long ago.

If only we two could be as one --
  There would be no room for dark clouds,
Only the radiant sun.

****

Love Decision

My angel, you look so closely at me; nearer
my lips are your words of tenderness and
warmth pulling me to you with your em-
bracing love.
Eyes beholding, -- I look to you, joyous
you are my friend, my lover; I need
ever to remain true.

Gazing into the pools of your mind,
searching within my feelings, I find,
your truth is our love.

****

on love...

Love is sporadic,
It comes and goes,
With nary a worry
As to hopes and dreams.

Everyone loves love
So sweet and cherished,
Ah, woe to them --
When love has perished.

****

Cherished Lover

His strength surpassed
all power and might,
But, gentle and tender
In the twilight night.

****

Forever Love

A star from the heavens
has fallen on thee,
and called thou my true love
Forever to be.

It twinkled so brightly
for all to see
My true love from heaven,
My true love and me.

****

Days

It soon is six o'clock I think
time to rise for food and drink,
new dawn awaits for me to pray --
ushering in a hope-filled day.

The sun shines brightly and
the Swallows are chirping --
The city awakes, amenities are spoken;
the plan of each day is laid with thought
progress fulfilling purpose.

As a smile crosses my face
readily with acceptance,
Lord, I am in love with life --
My Lord I love Thee.

****

Gifts of Lovers

Logs in the fireplace, flames ablaze glowing,
snow falls steadily, and warmth where we
are as mystery gifts beckon us curiously
beneath a majestic tree in resplendent dress.

Welcome Christmas! Our hearts find love
bestowed with music, joyously alive with
such the spirit that it brings to us.
The season spurs us affectionately, and
lovers softly kiss.

Outdoors children sleigh and caper.
Another log, another kiss -- you here by
my side, cookies and bells.

****

World Heartbeat

They were, they are, they will be.
Have crawled, have remained, may there
always live.
Days of youth -- there is today, the future,
each day.
Of leisure, of occupation, of family.
In anger, with laughter, to lament.
Those of wealth, some poor, others dead.

One is loved, despised are two -- all walk the
earth.
Compeers -- met in the lifetime.

****

Hedgecutter

I hear the motor of the hedgecutter
and I grow sad -- it reminds me of myself
without you, bits of me flying about,
becoming lost, dying.
I dare not allow it to happen,
I dare not miss you.
Enmeshed in dreams, how my senses tingle
and repine thinking of you,
the unreachable artificer.

****

Garden Night Reflections

The Dane from Tivoli
spoke of dad, toss offs
at the bar --
did it cause him to be glad?
Pillowed chairs drew him near
as Dane sipped, in cheer.
An address -- please write,
letters from Dane, I miss you
each night.
Entreating, "Come again to visit me,
I'm here for you at Tivoli."

****

Mind and I See

I wonder if through my tears
  my eyes see myself and understand
  what I feel when I experience the
  joy at an unexpected incident that
  occurs when I do not expect it.

However happy the tears might shine,
  I look into my thoughts behind the light
  and find support shielding shades
  of tears, and, prying words seem not
  to burn the spaces of my mind.

****

A Different Nourishment

Her agony intense, she is threatened
and abused, violated cruelly, painfully
scarred -- bloody aches evidence of the
marked plight that diminishes her to
neglect of herself while it foments
hate-filled, distressed suffering
which crowds her mind and, wrecks
her beauty.
The brutal deceiver kills her spirit and,
a love that sadly has consumed her.

Absorbed, she is cognizant he will
exist with the truth of her grace and
the resumption of a torn life
pieced together -- apart.

****

Vital Spark

Anger searching for calm, mooring no quiet --
stock thoughts of shadowed stillness,
secluded bearings, peace perhaps.
  Slatted carpenter bench empty, the
standing wood weathered aside supporting
poles hugging the dock of Brady,
  justly there -- blackened and chipped
  in the black summer night, inviting me.

Wind gusts rush the restless mind
  and body gripping, pulling fiercely,
come, enter the murky midnight sea.

Sudden blankness --
  encountered swift departure -- flight!
Fleeing, vanishing, escaping; -- heat rain
  palpates my skin as motors transmission
  the street and the splash of turning
  tires on the road whisper a welcome.

****

Naked Torment

She strikes the door.
At ten o'clock her time arrives --
She strikes the door!

Loose to the public she gesticulates
with unhappy and restless eyes.
Oh lady jester! not so humorous to yourself,
Not to act a sad role, to not entertain.

Along the floor the belly scrapes,
touching each tile with dirt from the
pulsating body once entombed in that
quiet hot room barren with heat,
empty with cold mattress,
unsheeted to cover the naked age.

Now and again, searching the tormented
faces everywhere for her missing man,
she finds herself -- not alone.

****

Untitled

I was there for everyone.
I grew weary and did not care
for myself.
I was lost and despaired.
Then, I remembered when I was
not lost; something special guides
me because I am there once again
as I was then -- for everyone,
especially for you.

****

And He Is Here

He comes to the food, then pecks
with caution -- ever aware, ever alert.
He stands proud and walks slowly
a distance.
I see his deformity -- a handicap?
Do I see a look of aloneness
in his eyes?
Observing I ponder, is that sadness a
habit of pity in myself; an understanding
smile comes to my face -- I am suddenly
enlightened.
Oh, wondrous bird of the universe,
with broken wing you fly away.

****

Parsnip Dreams

Counter coffee and tables laden,
bare for one, two, four or more.

Meringue   muffins   fruit --
      vodka martinis tip.

Phones, not near puddings --
      dessert yesterday?

Busy waiters and bustling waitresses
scan a Bayonne Bridge; new to many --
      complete with Alfonse.

Heart breakers dining and holding
conversation, perhaps over pork.

Vendors visit, no Moonie art.

A mind to play persons private two
drop coins that make music;
      kid chipmunk is free.

Wrestlers' photograph packs eyes at
you while Hibiscus filament bows
      color danger.

Money rolls in -- please don't scald,
noisy smiles dread not sipped coffee --
      "do dine downtown."

****

What You Do?

Dirty boy, dirty boy, dirty bad
tomata eater, you ate it -- was sweet?
Sweet dirty boy, tomata hungers juicy
seeds, dirty sweet boy.
Ripe love dirty boy -- sweet bad dirty
boy, you eat tomata.

****

Empty Horizon

I wish to wed everyone
I, weak trash to share
I cling from you, to you --
in love with each of you.
I, trampled proprietress
promising love -- solely for you,
wanton provider -- corrupt transgressor.

****

All I Want

I encountered you in the sky -- above all else
and sailed into friendly conversation
with you, a marathon runner -- we spoke of
prisoners and Western ranches.
Laughter was not scarce, you were handsome --
Colorado bound.

As flight attendants guarded through the
pillowed aisles, our non-stop chatting
clutched me at ease and telephone
designates were traded; I was happy --
Colorado bound.

You went to Denver, and the miles took me
to a distant expanse where cowboys in rodeos
on bronco competed and square dancing after
rafting held me poised for motion,
vigorous for woodland walks and
riding Stallion -- the miles shortened.

Now Autumn telephone talks, of a
New York October Run, yes, and more...

Dinner by the Summer sea, under Florida
moonlight, near you, and soft music.

****

The Meeting

As I studied your face quickly
that morning, I realized I'm
beginning to understand you.
You are there especially for me --
-- for us.

****

Diligent Dodger

I'm oo tirod and wish to rest my mind
to dream.
I reason I can't relax -- weariness and
too much writing.
Concoction of a topic that will not
direct double exhaustion and inability
to unwind on a subject penetrating,
engaging, poignant, decipherable
AND is easy to write.
Free verse or blank verse requires
organization and consistency and
will have to be comprehendible.

So! I am about to tell you what is,
and what comes following.
The subject matter to entertain you,
enlighten, perhaps it will be enjoyable
and pleasurable, to be read and reread --
a poem with pluck.

My desire for you is for just that.
Alas, my eyes are closing, and the
pen is scrawling, I know only slumber.

****